W9-BSQ-155

# LIVING CREATURES IN THE HOLY QUR'AN

Written and Illustrated by

# Shahada Sharelle Abdul Haqq

Published by Tughra Books

335 Clifton Ave.

Clifton, NJ 07011 USA

www.tughrabooks.com

ISBN 1-59784-930-8

# CONTENTS

# INTRODUCTION

The Holy Qur'an encourages us to be compassionate to all animals. From ants to elephants we must respect all creatures no matter how big or small, for they are all God's creatures too.

'*...No living creature is there moving on the Earth, no bird flying on its two wings, but they are communities like you. We have neglected nothing in the Book (the Qur'an)...*' (Qur'an 6:38)

Wolves, snakes, horses, cows, sheep, fish and dogs are just a few of the animals that feature in the stories of the prophets in the Holy Qur'an. God even gave one prophet the special and unique gift of being able to understand and communicate with animals, birds and insects. Other animals, such as bees, spiders, moths, donkeys and lions don't feature in stories but they are used to teach us a lesson and they each have a special mention in the Holy Qur'an. In this book, we have collected together some of those short lessons and longer stories for you to enjoy.

With each story or lesson, there is a reference giving the number of the chapter and the particular verse or verses in which the creature is mentioned.

With the exception of the first one, all the stories in this book are in the order of the chapters in the Qur'an. Please also remember that it is incumbent on believers to offer prayers to all the messengers of God after their names are mentioned by saying "peace and blessings be upon them."

# 1
# ALL CREATURES

## Prophet Noah
## and the Ark

**(Qur'an 11:40-41 & 23:27)**

Prophet Noah lived during a time when people had begun to worship idols. They made statues of good, honest, well-respected people, who had once lived among them. Then, after a time, they began to worship them. Noah told them to return to worshipping God, the one true God. He warned them that there would be a terrible punishment if they did not. "O my people," he said, "worship God. There is no other god but Him."

Nobody listened to Noah. They didn't care about God or the way He wanted them to live, and they began to be selfish and unkind to their neighbors.

Prophet Noah was a good man and he was very calm and patient. He tried hard to get people to listen to him, and his words of warning touched the hearts of the common worker, the weak and the poor. Unfortunately, however, the rich and the powerful, the influential leaders and the mighty rulers disliked what Noah had to say. "Why should we listen to him?" they asked. "He's just a man like us. He is a liar."

Hour after hour, day after day for nine hundred and fifty years, this patient Prophet preached to his people, asking them to worship none other than God the Cherisher and Sustainer of the worlds. Sadly, Noah saw that the number of believers was not increasing, and that the number of disbelievers was growing steadily. He was sad for his people, but he never reached the point of despair.

Then came a day when God revealed to Noah that no others would believe. God encouraged him not to grieve for the disbelievers, for they would spread corruption and disbelief throughout the land. It was then, that Noah prayed that the wicked people be destroyed. "My Lord, leave not one of the disbelievers on the Earth," he said. "If you leave them, they will mislead Your followers and they will give birth to more wicked disbelievers."

God accepted Noah's prayers. Then, God told Noah that there was going to be a great flood, and He instructed him to build a large boat which was called an ark. And so with God's knowledge and with help from the angels, Noah chose a place outside the city to build the ark. To everybody's amusement, the place he chose was miles away from the sea. People came to watch him work on the boat and they mocked him. "What good is a boat so far from the sea!" they said. Noah told them what God had said about the flood, but they just laughed and walked on.

"Soon you'll understand why I'm building this boat," Noah said, as he worked on. Finally, the ark was completed and Noah sat and waited for God's command. One day, God revealed these words to Noah. "When water miraculously gushes from the oven in your home, that will be a sign that the flood has begun and you must act."

When that terrible day arrived, Noah hurried to open up the ark, and he summoned his family and the believers to board the ark. He had also gathered a pair, male and female, of every kind of animal, bird and insect on the Earth, and two by two, they entered the ark. The disbelievers laughed out loud as they watched Noah lead these creatures onto the ark. "You must be out of your mind, Noah," they cried. "What are you going to do with all those animals?"

Now, sadly, Noah's wife was not a believer, so she did not join him on the ark, and neither did one of his sons. He was secretly a disbeliever, but had pretended faith in front of his father, Noah.

When all the animals were safely on the ark, the water began to rise from the cracks in the earth and it rained down from the sky in torrents. Day after day, it continued to rain heavily. The water grew deeper and deeper, and soon vast areas of land were underwater. The water lifted the ark from its resting place, and it sailed safely on with its precious crew. Still the rain beat down and the water rose higher and higher till it covered hills and high land. From the ark, Noah could see his son on a mountainside. He called out to him, pleading with him to join them on the ark.

"No, Father," he said. "I'll climb to the top of this high mountain and wait there. That will save me from the flood."

"There is no savior from God's will, except for him on whom God has mercy," cried Noah. Then a great wave rose between the two men, and Noah's son was drowned. The water rose and rose until everywhere and everything was covered. Nobody and nothing could survive.

Time passed and finally the earth swallowed up the water and the sky held back the rain. The will of God had been fulfilled. The people of Noah had been destroyed and the flood had cleansed the Earth of disbelievers. The ark came to rest on Mount Judi and the water receded. It was finally safe to leave the ark. Noah opened the doors and the animals, birds and insects all scrambled off the ark. Noah, his family and the believers were happy to be on dry land again and they thanked God for keeping them safe.

It was said, "Away with the people who worship anything other than the one true God."

***In the end, every living creature on Earth will submit to God, either by choice or by God's will. There is no doubt.***

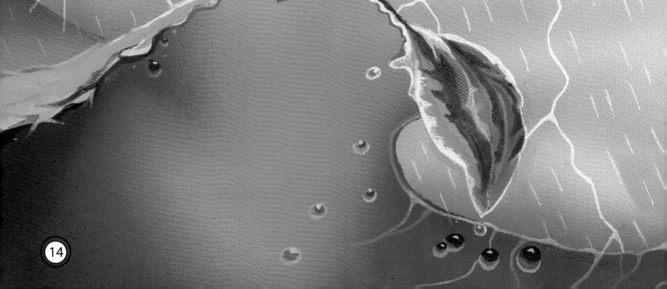

# 2
# COWS

## The Story of the Yellow Cow
### (Qur'an 2:67-73)

God devoted an entire chapter of the Holy Qur'an to teach mankind this important lesson. The story takes place during the lifetime of Prophet Moses.

Among the Israelites, at that time, there lived a good and pious man. He was a poor man but he lived his life earning an honest living. He did everything for the sake of God and never for selfish gain.

His very last words on his death bed were, "O God, I place my wife, my little son and my only possession, a calf, in your care." Then, for safe keeping, he asked his wife to lead the calf into the forest and leave it there for God to take care of.

A few years later, when the boy had grown up, his mother told him about the calf.

"Your father left you a calf in the trust of God," she said. "It must have grown into a cow by now."

The young man was pleasantly surprised, to hear about the calf. "Where is it?" he asked his mother.

"Your father always used to say, 'I trust in God.' before he did anything. Do as he did," his mother replied. "Then go and look for the cow."

With a rope in his hand, the young man walked into the forest and prostrated himself before God. "O God, Lord of Abraham, Jacob and Job, peace be upon them, please return my father's cow to me," he said. Then, when he raised his head, he saw a cow walking towards him. It stopped submissively beside him. He stroked its face, and then he tied the rope around its neck and lead it home.

From that day on, the cow wouldn't let anyone else come near it, except for this young man. The young man, who was a woodcutter, was as pious as his father. Whatever he earned from chopping wood, he divided into three equal portions. He gave the first portion to his mother, the second to himself and the third to charity.

Now about this time, a man was murdered. The people wanted to find out who had committed this terrible crime so they went to Prophet Moses to ask for his help in seeking God's guidance.

Moses instructed them to slaughter a cow. "Then," he said, "you must strike the dead body with a piece of the cow and this will reveal who the murderer is."

"Is this a joke, Moses?" they asked. "Are you making fun of us?"

"God forbid," said Moses. "I would never do anything so foolish."

"But what type of cow should we slaughter?" they asked.

"The cow should be neither too old nor too young," replied Moses. "Now go and do as you've been asked."

In fact, it didn't matter what type of cow they slaughtered. However, they persisted in arguing over the matter, and they asked Moses more pointless questions.

"What color should the cow be?" asked one.

"Yellow," replied Moses.

Still unsatisfied, they asked for more details about the cow.

"Very well," said Moses. "You should find an unyoked cow – one that doesn't plough the soil or water the fields. Oh and there shouldn't be any blemishes on it at all."

And so the people went out in search of this special cow. The only one that matched the description was the yellow cow owned by the young man. As soon as they saw the cow, they knew they had to have it and they asked the young man how much he would sell it for.

"I'll have to consult my mother on the matter, first," he said. So they accompanied him to his house, and they offered his mother three gold coins for the cow. She refused their coins saying the cow was worth much more.

They increased their offer several times, and the young man's mother refused each new offer. "You must ask your mother to be reasonable," they said.

"I won't sell the cow without my mother's approval," the young man replied. "Even if you offered me its hide filled with gold, I wouldn't sell it to you without her approval."

When his mother heard this, she smiled and said, "Let that be the price. You will pay us its hide filled with gold," she said.

The men decided that no other cow would do. They had to have that yellow cow at any price, and so they agreed to pay for it with its hide filled with gold.

Finally, they obeyed God and slaughtered the yellow cow. The man's body was struck with a piece of the cow. Then, by the will of God, the man was brought back to life, long enough to tell them who had murdered him.

It would not have mattered which cow they had slaughtered. Any cow would have done. Their stubbornness and resistance to obey, had resulted in them asking Prophet Moses a lot of unnecessary questions, and so God had made the task unnecessarily difficult for them.

*Immediate submission to God is its own reward.*

# 3
# DONKEYS

## The Miracle of a Man and His Donkey Brought Back to Life
### (Qur'an 2:259)

A wise man called Ezra was once travelling on his donkey when he came to the ruined city of Jerusalem. King Nebuchadnezzar had destroyed the city and killed many of its citizens.

As Ezra rode through the rubble, he thought to himself, "How will God ever bring this dead city to life again?"

God willed to show him, so he put Ezra to sleep for one hundred years. At the end of the one hundred years, he brought him back to life again.

While Ezra slept, the city of Jerusalem was rebuilt. People moved into the city and they started to live there again. The years passed, the population increased, and the city flourished. The children of Israel moved back into the city.

God sent an angel to revive Ezra's heart and his sight so that he could feel and see how God revives the dead. When his resurrection was complete, God asked him, "How long did you sleep for?"

Ezra looked up at the sun. "Perhaps for a day or half a day," he replied, for he knew he had gone to sleep early in the afternoon and it was then late afternoon, so he thought that it was the same day.

"O no," said the angel, "you've been asleep for a hundred years. Look at your food and your drink, they show no signs of change." Ezra looked at the basket of grapes, figs, and fruit juice. They were all just as he had left them. Nothing was spoiled or rotten. The donkey, however had died and all that was left of him were dry bones. God brought the animal back to life before Ezra's eyes.

"I know now that God has power over all things," exclaimed Ezra when he witnessed this miracle.

*We must understand that all of life is a miracle from God.*
*Time is nothing to Him. He is above His creation. He need*
*only to say 'be' and it is.*

# 4
# BIRDS

## Prophet Abraham and the Tamed Birds
### (Qur'an 2:260)

Prophet Abraham, the father of many prophets, once went into the wilderness, and there he asked God a question. "My Lord, show me how you give life to the dead."

"Why? Do you not believe?" God asked him.

"Yes, I do believe," replied Abraham, "but I'm asking you to show me so I can be sure in my heart."

"Very well," said God and he ordered Abraham to train four birds to come back to him when he called them. Once they had been trained, he was to cut the four birds into parts, and to place the parts of the birds on different hills. When this had been done, he was to call the birds to him again.

Prophet Abraham did all this and when he called the birds, they returned to him quickly. Miraculously, their bodies were whole again. The power of God had been shown to Abraham and he believed in it with both his mind and his heart.

He learnt that, without a doubt, when God says, 'Be', what God wants comes immediately into existence.

***Only God can bring the dead back to life.***

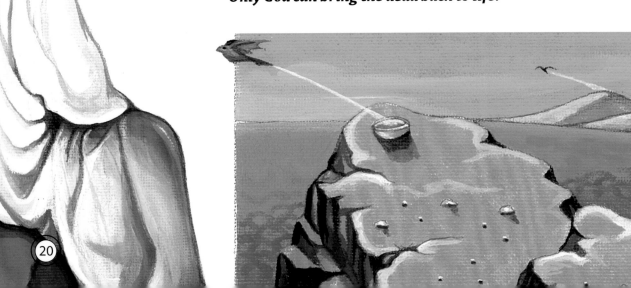

# Prophet Jesus and the Clay Bird
## (Qur'an 3:49)

God allowed His messengers to perform miracles so that people will believe in Him. Once, when Prophet Jesus was sitting amongst the people, he said, "I will bring you a sign from your Lord." He then took a handful of clay and asked, "Shall I make a live bird for you?"

"Are you able to do that?" they asked.

"Yes, by the will of my Lord," he replied. He then took the clay and shaped it to resemble a bird. Next, he blew upon it saying, "By the will of God, be a living bird."

Then, before their eyes, the lump of clay became a living bird. It spread its wings and flew up into the sky. By God's will, Prophet Jesus was also able to bring sight to people born blind. He could heal lepers and wake the dead. Surely this was a sign for people to believe.

***God's prophets are able to perform miracles but only with the help of God.***

# 5
# CALVES

## The Golden Calf
### (Qur'an 4:153)

After having freed the Israelites from the wicked Egyptian pharaoh, Prophet Moses and his brother, Prophet Aaron, were led to Mount Sinai. Moses left his people at the foot of the mountain in the care of his brother Aaron. "Take my place among my people. Lead them in the right way of obeying and worshipping God alone, and keep them united," Moses told his brother.

Moses stayed at the top of the mountain for more than thirty days and nights. Some of his people became restless for they did not know that God had extended his time by another ten days to forty days. Samiri, an evil trouble-maker, took advantage of this restlessness, and he suggested that the people found themselves another guide. "Moses has broken his promise to you," he told them. "To find true guidance, you need a new god, and I shall provide one for you."

Samiri was an experienced goldsmith, so he was able to collect a large amount of gold jewellery and ornaments from the people. He melted them all down and made a golden calf. When the golden calf was completed, it made a strange whistling sound as if the wind was blowing through its hollow structure. It was almost as if it had a spirit of its own.

Samiri presented the golden calf to the people. "Here is your real god," he said. "Forget what Moses and Aaron have told you. Their God can't help you."

Since the people had in the past been very superstitious, they quickly linked the strange sound coming from the calf to something supernatural, and unfortunately some of the people began to worship this golden idol.

Prophet Aaron was very patient. He tried very hard to make the misled people understand that Samiri was an evil, wicked magician, and that the worship of idols was against the teachings of Moses. Prophet Aaron's preaching, however, had no effect on the straying and misguided people. They continued to fall deeper and deeper into disbelief.

***We must be patient in our belief.***

# 6
# PIGS

## (Qur'an 5:3)

There are certain types of meat that God has forbidden us to eat. We mustn't eat the meat of animals found dead and not killed by men, the flesh of pigs and the flesh of any animals slaughtered in the name of anyone other than God. However, if a person is close to starving and there is nothing else to eat except for pork, he or she is allowed to eat pork, for God is forgiving and merciful. However, when starvation is no longer a concern, he or she must stop eating this forbidden meat.

*What God has forbidden, no man can make lawful.*

# 7
# RAVENS

## The Raven and the First Murder
### (Qur'an 5:27-31)

This story begins with Prophet Adam and his wife Eve, the mother and father of all mankind. Abel and Cain were their two sons.

Abel, the younger of the two sons was a friendly, cheerful and God-fearing young man. Cain, on the other hand, was selfish, ill-tempered and jealous. When the two boys grew up, Cain became a farmer and Abel became a shepherd.

Then a dispute arose between Abel and Cain. To reach an agreement, it was decided that each one of the young men should offer a sacrifice to God.

Abel offered a fat lamb, the best of his flock to God, and Cain offered a sheaf of the very worst of his corn. Then, they both waited for a reply. God sent a white fire that consumed Abel's offering. Cain's offering was not accepted. God had given Abel his blessing.

Cain was very jealous and he grew angry. His jealousy towards Abel allowed Satan to control him and he decided to kill his brother.

"If you stretch forth your hand to kill me, then it is not for me to stretch forth my hand to kill you, because I fear God the cherisher of the worlds," Abel told Cain. "I intend to let you take upon yourself my sin as well as yours, for you will be among the companions of the hell fire that is the punishment for those who do wrong."

This only made Cain angrier. He picked up a stone and hit his innocent brother on the head with it. Abel died, and Cain didn't know what to do with his brother's dead body. Nobody had had to bury anybody before. Cain wandered around aimlessly, carrying his brother's dead body on his shoulder, not knowing where to hide it.

Finally, God sent a raven, black as night, to show him. Cain sat watching as two ravens had a fight with each other. One pecked the other to death. Then, with its beak and claws, it began to dig a small pit in the ground. It placed the dead bird in the pit and covered it with earth. Then it flew away.

Cain understood that this was a sign from God. This was how he was to dispose of his brother's body. "Woe is me," said Cain. "I could not hide my shame as this raven has done." Then he became full of regret for the terrible thing he had done.

*To take the life of one person is to take the life of all mankind,*
*and to save the life of one person is to save the life of all mankind.*

# 8
# LOCUSTS

## A Plague of Locusts
### (Qur'an 7:133)

Once, a powerful pharaoh ruled Egypt and this pharaoh was very cruel to the descendants of Jacob, known as the Israelites. They were kept in slavery and forced to work for him for little or no pay. The Egyptians worshipped and obeyed this pharaoh and they carried out his orders.

God in his infinite mercy sent Prophet Moses and his brother Aaron to tell Pharaoh to release the Israelites from slavery, and to let them go free.

Even after witnessing several miracles performed by Moses, by the grace of God, Pharaoh still refused to humble himself before the Lord and he would not release the Israelites.

Moses prayed to God, and God sent a swarm of locusts. The locusts covered the ground so that not one inch of soil could be seen. Then, they began to eat all the crops growing in the fields and all the fruit on the trees. Soon nothing green remained – not a tree, not a plant, not a leaf in the whole of Egypt. The locusts devoured everything.

The people of Egypt begged Moses to ask God to stop the plague of locusts. Pharaoh summoned Moses to him. "Pray to the Lord your God to stop this deadly plague and I promise to allow the Israelites to leave Egypt with you."

Moses left Pharaoh and prayed to God. God changed the direction of the wind, and it carried the locusts to the Red Sea. Soon there was not a single locust left in Egypt. The locusts had departed, but Pharaoh did not fulfill his promise. He did not let the Israelites leave Egypt.

***Arrogance within a man's heart is not pleasing to God.***

# 9
# LICE

## A Plague of Lice
### (Qur'an 7:133)

In the time of Prophet Moses, God had sent a severe drought and a devastating famine as a sign to the people of Egypt to mend their ways. He had also sent a plague of locusts that had eaten everything in their path. These were all clear signs of God's existence, and yet, still the people had disbelieved.

Each time they said, "O Moses, appeal to your Lord for us. Tell Him that if He removes the punishment from us, we shall indeed believe in Him, and let the Israelites go with you."

Then each time God removed the punishment, they broke their word. Pharaoh and his followers had grown so arrogant and become so defiant in their disbelief, that God sent a plague of lice to spread disease amongst those who refused to listen to Prophet Moses' advice.

*The safest and most sensible path for all people in the world is to obey God and His blessed prophets.*

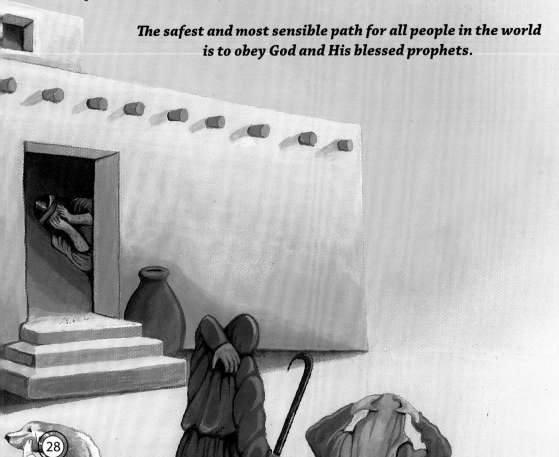

# 10
# WEEVILS

## A Plague of Weevils
### (Qur'an 7:133)

The people of Prophet Moses' time refused to listen to the message of truth he brought to them. They received a series of five divine punishments. One of these punishments was an invasion of weevils. These tiny insects ate their ripened crops, destroyed their stores of grain and irritated their skin causing great misery.

Finally, the people begged Prophet Moses to pray for them and to ask God to relieve them from this terrible punishment.

Feeling pity, Prophet Moses prayed and asked God for help. The punishment was lifted but the people did not show gratitude to God and they soon went back to their disobedient ways.

*Disobedience of God's commands results in punishment.*

# 11
# FROGS

## The Exodus from Egypt
## and the Parting of the Red Sea
### (Qur'an 07:133)

God in His infinite mercy sent Prophet Moses and his brother Aaron to tell Pharaoh to free the Israelites from slavery. This message greatly angered Pharaoh. Because of his stubborn disbelief and oppression of the Israelites, God sent down plagues. First, God sent the floods. Torrents of rain battered the land and destroyed all growing crops and fruit. Then came the black cloud of locusts, then the lice, the termites, and the weevils. Still Pharaoh would not believe and his heart grew harder. Next, God sent a plague of frogs. They hopped around people's homes and into their beds. People were scared to open their mouths in case the frogs hopped in. Pharaoh begged Moses to take them away. Moses told him that there was more trouble to come if he did not let the Israelites go. The arrogant pharaoh still refused to listen to Moses. Then, the River Nile turned blood-red and there was no water to drink, but still the stubborn pharaoh refused to listen. God told Moses to leave Egypt with his family and the Israelites. Pharaoh still tried to stop them and he sent his army after them.

They came to the shore of the Red Sea. The sea was in front of them and the soldiers were behind them. They were terrified.

"You've no need to be afraid," said Moses. "There's no doubt that God is with me and He will help us."

Then God guided Moses to strike the water with his staff. Suddenly, the waves parted and a dry path appeared in front of them. Moses and the Israelites were able to walk along the seabed and cross safely to the other side. Pharaoh and his soldiers quickly followed the Israelites, but Moses waved his staff again and God caused the sea to flow back, drowning Pharaoh and his soldiers. Safe on the far shore, the Israelites escaped to freedom with Moses and Aaron.

'We plagued them with the flood, the locusts, the lice, the termites and the weevils, the frogs and the river of blood, but even after all these signs, they still refused to believe and they broke their promise to set the Israelites free.'

*There is a painful punishment for those who do not obey God and His messengers.*

# 12
# CAMELS

## Prophet Salih and the She-Camel
### (Qur'an 11:64-65)

Prophet Salih lived around 2,400 BC. He was born among the Thamud people of the ancient Arabian Peninsula, who, like the Ad people before them, were blessed with the skills to build huge stone palaces and carve out beautiful homes from the rocks in the mountains.

Salih was extremely wise and good-natured, and the people of Thamud relied on him for his good judgment. "O Salih," they said, "you've been a figure of hope to us and we wanted to make you our chief, until you asked us to leave our gods and worship only your God." They were arrogant and selfish and Salih warned them that they were doomed if they did not mend their sinful ways.

Seeing that more and more people began to believe Salih, the chieftains began to worry. They wanted Salih to stop preaching. "Prove to us that you really are the messenger of God by performing a miracle," they said. "Ask your Lord to make a she-camel. The she-camel must be ten months pregnant, tall and graceful and she should come out from the rock."

So Prophet Salih prayed to God to grant their request. God then ordered a

distant rock to split open bringing forth a tall and graceful she-camel which was ten months pregnant. This miracle happened before their eyes and they were amazed.

God had sent the she-camel to the people of Al-Hijr, the rocky tract. It was a blessed camel, and its milk was distributed to thousands of men, women and children. It was obvious to everyone that it was not an ordinary camel, but a sign from God.

At first, people allowed the she-camel to drink at the spring and graze freely. After a while, however, the disbelievers began to complain about the camel. "It frightens our cattle and it drinks all the water and leaves none for our animals," they said.

Prophet Salih feared that they might kill her, so he warned them, "My people, this she-camel is a sign of God to you. Leave her to graze in peace on God's Earth. Do not harm her or you will be punished."

Sadly, one day, as the she-camel went to drink at the spring, it was shot in the leg by an arrow. It tried desperately to escape but it was hampered by the arrow and it was brutally killed.

"You may enjoy life for three more days, then you will be punished," Prophet Salih warned the men. Salih hoped that before the end of the third day they would see the folly of their ways and ask for God's forgiveness, but instead they laughed at Salih. "Why wait three days?" they asked. "Let the punishment come sooner."

Salih pleaded with them. "My people, why are you so eager to do evil rather than good." The disbelievers also plotted to kill Prophet Salih and those in his household. Before this could happen, however, Prophet Salih, his family and some of the believers left the town.

Three days after Salih's warning, a series of mighty thunderbolts filled the sky, and a huge earthquake followed, that destroyed the entire Thamud tribe and its homeland. Neither their strong stone buildings, nor their rock-hewn homes could protect them. Only Salih and the just and righteous believers were saved.

"O my people!" cried Prophet Salih. "I conveyed to you the message of my Lord, and I gave you good advice, but it seems you do not like good advisors."

**None has the right to be worshipped but God the Creator of all things.**

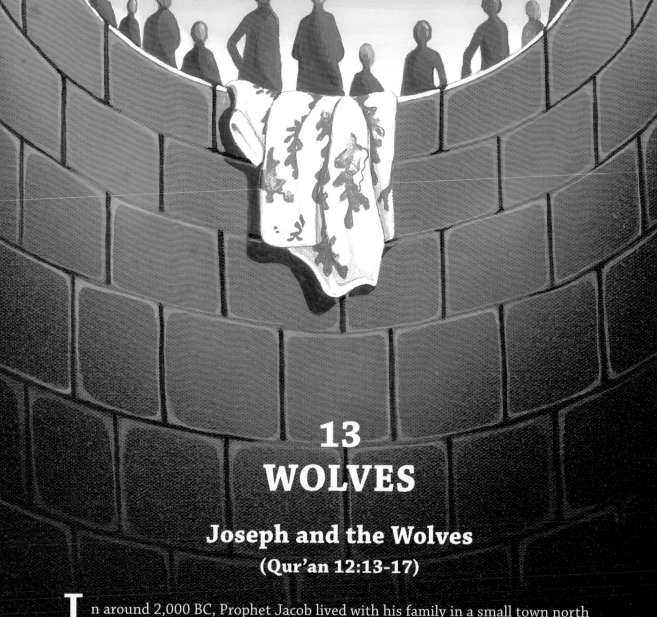

# 13
# WOLVES

## Joseph and the Wolves
### (Qur'an 12:13-17)

In around 2,000 BC, Prophet Jacob lived with his family in a small town north of Syria called Canaan. God had blessed Prophet Jacob with twelve sons and a daughter. His two youngest sons, Joseph and Benjamin, were the sons of his beloved second wife, Rachel. Joseph was a confident, intelligent, good-natured boy and he was strong and handsome. He was Jacob's favorite son.

One day, Joseph said to Prophet Jacob, "Father I had a strange dream last night. In my dream, the sun, the moon and eleven stars bowed down before me!"

His father was afraid by the dream. "Son, don't tell your brothers about this vision or they may plot against you," he warned Joseph.

Joseph's brothers were jealous of the love and affection their father showed him, so one day, they plotted to kill Joseph. They begged their father to let him go out into the woods with them so he could play and enjoy himself.

"Joseph is too young to go to the woods," said Jacob. "A wild wolf might run off with him."

This planted the seed of an idea in the brothers' minds. They asked Jacob again and again to let Joseph go with them, promising to look after him. Finally, Jacob gave in, and against his better judgment, he let Joseph go with his brothers into the woods.

Once in the woods, the brothers took off Joseph's shirt and pushed him into a well. Joseph cried out and begged them to help him out of the well, but his cruel brothers just walked off and left their younger brother alone and afraid in the deep dark well.

They smeared the blood from a wild animal on Joseph's shirt and went to their father weeping. "Father," they said, "We were having a race and we left Joseph with our things. Whilst we were gone, a wolf attacked him. Here's his shirt. We found it covered with blood but we couldn't find Joseph. The wolf must have eaten him."

Deep down in his heart, Prophet Jacob knew his sons were lying, but he could see that the bloody shirt had been torn, perhaps by a wild wolf or wolves. This noble prophet, however, showed patience and didn't complain. He remembered it was best only to seek help from God.

Not long after, a caravan of traders arrived at the well looking for water. They found Joseph and they took him to Egypt. There they sold him in the market to one of Pharaoh's ministers. The minister was a kind master and he raised Joseph as a son.

God gave Joseph full prophethood, and He also gave him a special gift. Joseph could interpret dreams. His gift helped him to become the keeper of the grain and the second in command over the land of Egypt. After many years, he was able to send for his family, and they travelled from Canaan to Egypt. When Joseph received his family, he was sitting on his throne. His family all bowed down before him and Joseph remembered his dream.

"O Father, this is the dream I told you about," said Joseph. "The dream where I saw the sun (my father), the moon (my mother) and eleven stars (my brothers) bow down before me. My Lord has made it come true. God is the most generous and kind. Truly, He is the All-Knowing, the All-Wise."

The father and son embraced each other affectionately and shed many tears over their long separation. "Now that I've seen your face again, I can die in peace," said Jacob.

***Avoid seeking revenge and be patient,
for God is the best avenger.***

# 14
# ANGELS

**(Qur'an 13:22-24, 35:1 & 32:11)**

Angels are very important in Islam. In fact, believing in angels is one of the six articles of faith in Islam. There are more angels than any other creature in God's creation. They only do things God assigns them to do – which include recording the good and bad deeds of human beings, receiving the souls of the dying, and guarding Heaven and Hell.

Angels are beautiful beings made of light, so that they can assume any shape. They are described as having wings. Some have two wings, some have four wings, and some eight wings. It is said that Angel Gabriel, the most powerful of all the angels, has 600 wings.

Angels do not eat, drink or sleep, and they do not ever grow older, although, like all of God's creations, they will die one day. The will of the angels is purely to please God and to do His will. Day and night they give praise to God and they never grow tired. Angels possess great powers given to them by God. They are messengers from God, and Angel Gabriel is the most important of these messengers.

Angel Gabriel was responsible for revealing the Qur'an to Prophet Muhammad, verse by verse, in a cave called Hira, near Mecca in Arabia on the night of Laylat al-Qadr, the Night of Divine Destiny. He appeared to the Prophet in both human and angel form.

Angels also visited Abraham in human form. Similarly, angels came to Lot to deliver him from danger in the form of handsome, young men.

As well as Angel Gabriel, there are other angels in the Qur'an who have names. Angel Michael is often depicted as the archangel of mercy and sustenance, who is responsible for bringing rain to Earth. He has helper angels who assist him in directing the winds and clouds, and with this help, food and clothing is provided for mankind. He is also responsible for rewarding people who have lived good lives.

Angel Azrael is the angel of death. He is responsible for releasing the soul from the physical body.

God is merciful and loving and in times of unhappiness, He sends Angel Ratail to relieve our sadness. Angel Ridwan is in charge of Paradise and Angel Maalik guards over the fires of Hell.

Each angel has been given a different task to perform. There are angels who distribute the rain and angels who drive the winds and the clouds. Then there are guardian angels responsible for protecting the believer throughout his life, at home or travelling, asleep or awake. There are two guardian angels for every believer. They are called Kiraman Katibin, which means "honorable scribes." One of them, Raqib, sits on the right shoulder and records good deeds, and the other, Atid, sits on the left and records bad deeds for Judgment Day. After every prayer, the believer greets each of these angels with the words, 'May the peace and blessings of God be with you.'

Some angels roam the world in search of gatherings where God is remembered. Some angels make up God's heavenly army, and standing in rows, they never get tired or sit down. Others bow or prostrate themselves in worship of God, and never raise their heads. No angel ever disobeys God.

**Believe in the unseen.**

# 15
# JINNS

## (Qur'an 15:27, 51:56, 15:18 & 72:1-20)

Before He created mankind, God created the race of jinns from smokeless flames of fire. Jinns are beings with free will who live on Earth in a parallel world to mankind. We cannot see them. They eat, drink, marry, have children and die the same as we do, but their lifespan is far longer than ours. They too will be present on the Day of Judgment and they too will either go to Paradise or Hell.

What makes them different from mankind are their powers and abilities. These were given to them as a test. If they oppress or mislead mankind from the guidance of God, they will be held accountable. Through knowing their powers, we can make sense of the mysteries around us. They are shape-shifters, meaning that they can take on any physical form they like, such as that of another human being, an animal or even a tree. They live for thousands of years and can travel long distances in a matter of seconds.

Using their powers of flying and invisibility, some evil jinns have taken part in occult activities. Before the time of Prophet Muhammad, fortune tellers were very accurate in their predictions. After the Prophet's arrival with the Holy Qur'an, the heavens were heavily guarded by angels, and any jinns who tried to listen were attacked by meteors or shooting stars.

Every human being is assigned a jinn called a *Qareen* which means 'constant companion'. It is this jinn who whispers to our base desires and constantly tries to divert us from righteousness. He pushes us to do evil things and to disobey God. Prophet Muhammad said, "Every single one of us has been assigned a companion from among the jinns."

"Even you, O messenger of God?" the companions of the Prophet asked.

"Even me," replied Prophet Muhammad, "but the difference is that God has helped me to battle against the jinn and he has submitted to God. Now he the jinn only tells me to do good."

We know that the Prophet preached to a group of jinns and they became believers. They saw Him as their Lord and Sustainer. Then they went back to their people and said, "We have heard a most wonderful recital which gives guidance towards righteousness so we believe in it, and we shall not join in the worship of any gods but our Lord. And exalted is the majesty of our Lord for He has taken neither a wife nor a son."

God has revealed an entire chapter dedicated to the invisible jinns, *Al-Jinn (The Jinn)*.

*The devotees of God will be protected from the curse of the jinns' evil whispers.*

# 16
# BEES

## (Qur'an 16:68-69)

*'God taught the bee to make its beehive in the mountains, in trees and also in man-made structures. Then, He taught them through instinct to suck (nectar) from all the fruit and flowers of the Earth, and to travel along the paths of the Lord which have been made easy for the bee to follow. There comes out from their bodies, a drink of varying colors (honey), which contains healing for mankind. Surely, in this there is a sign for people who think and reflect.'*

God has given the bee a very unique job. This little buzzing insect with four wings and six legs produces a delicious honey both for itself and for us to eat.

Bees live in large colonies of up to fifty thousand bees called a hive. With their incredible engineering skills, the bees build a honeycomb inside the hive. The honeycomb has many hexagonal or six-sided cells made of a special wax which comes from the body of the bee. Each bee in the beehive has a special job to do. Not all bees make honey and the bees that do make honey have to work very hard. They will visit around a hundred flowers in one trip and it will take around five hundred and fifty bees to produce just under half a kilogram of honey. In fact, one bee will only produce a twelfth of a teaspoon of honey in its lifetime.

The honey-producing bee has a special dance she performs when she finds a flower with a good source of nectar. She quickly flies back to her hive with the happy news. She then performs a special 'waggle' dance. The other bees understand at once, the meaning of this special dance, and they swarm off with the finder bee to the flowers. They each suck the nectar, the sugary juice, from the heart of the flowers or fruit blossom. The nectar is stored in their special stomachs, ready to be transferred to the honey-making bees in the hive. The honey bees have glands which produce an enzyme. The enzyme is mixed with the nectar in the bee's mouth. Then it is dropped into the hexagonal-shaped cells of the honeycomb. The bees then cover the cells with a protective wax coating which they make themselves. The nectar thickens and it turns into a sweet honey.

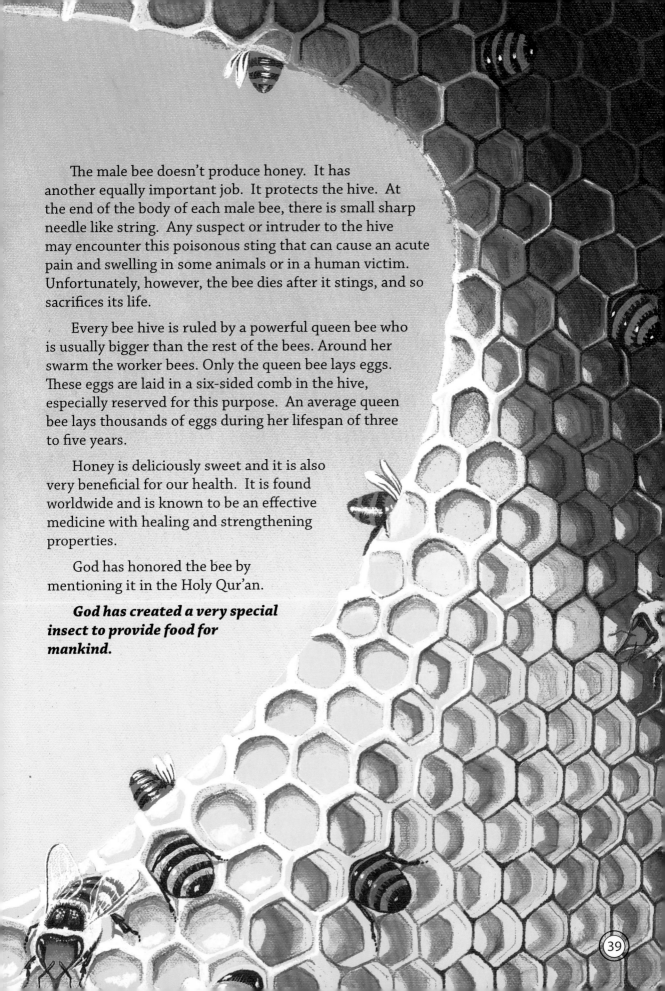

The male bee doesn't produce honey. It has another equally important job. It protects the hive. At the end of the body of each male bee, there is small sharp needle like string. Any suspect or intruder to the hive may encounter this poisonous sting that can cause an acute pain and swelling in some animals or in a human victim. Unfortunately, however, the bee dies after it stings, and so sacrifices its life.

Every bee hive is ruled by a powerful queen bee who is usually bigger than the rest of the bees. Around her swarm the worker bees. Only the queen bee lays eggs. These eggs are laid in a six-sided comb in the hive, especially reserved for this purpose. An average queen bee lays thousands of eggs during her lifespan of three to five years.

Honey is deliciously sweet and it is also very beneficial for our health. It is found worldwide and is known to be an effective medicine with healing and strengthening properties.

God has honored the bee by mentioning it in the Holy Qur'an.

**God has created a very special insect to provide food for mankind.**

# 17
# DOGS

## The Companions of the Cave and their Dog, Qitmir
### (Qur'an 18:18)

In the third century AD, there lived a ruthless Emperor named Decianus who worshipped idols in the city of Ephesus, one of the outposts of the Roman Empire. Emperor Decianus insisted that his subjects worshipped his idols and he tortured and killed anyone who worshipped anything other than his false gods. The legend says that there were several young men living in the palace who believed in only one God as taught by Prophet Jesus. Decianus demanded that they denounce their faith but they refused to. Secure in the love of God, they stood before their people and proclaimed, "Our Lord is the only Lord of the Heavens and the Earth so we will never call upon any god but Him, for in doing so we would have told a terrible lie."

They were important men, so Emperor Decianus delayed his decision on their case and he left the town on business. While he was away, the young men, fearing for their lives, decided to seek refuge in a nearby cave. They took their faithful dog, Qitmir with them.

When Decianus returned, he was furious to learn of their escape and he was determined to capture and punish the young men. He sent his soldiers to find them, and learning that the young men were staying in a cave, he ordered his troops to seal them inside.

Instead of dying a slow death, God in His mercy allowed the young men to remain in a peaceful sleep for three hundred and nine years. Their dog Qitmir fell asleep too. With his two forelegs stretched out in front of him, he lay across the entrance to the cave like a guard dog.

One day, a shepherd, looking for some shelter for his herd of goats and sheep, decided to remove the rocks sealing the entrance to the cave. This disturbed the young men and their dog.

God raised them from their sleep, and they woke up.
At first they were disorientated.

"How long have we been here for?" asked one. "We've
been here for half a day or a day at the most," replied another.

"Only God knows how long we've been here," they concluded.

Then realizing how hungry they all were, they decided that one of them should go
to the town and buy some food. They collected together the silver coins that they had
between them. Then, they sent Yamlika to Ephesus. Yamlika was warned to be careful
and courteous so as not to attract any undue attention to himself. "If they realize
who you are," warned the others, "they will stone you to death or make you return to
their way of worship."

As he entered the town, Yamlika was amazed to discover everything had changed
from when he had last visited it. He also saw that the people were no longer
oppressed and the belief in one God was practised openly.

When Yamlika presented his antique silver coins with Decianus's head on them,
the shopkeeper was surprised. He wondered whether there was some hidden treasure
somewhere, that the young man had stumbled across. The shopkeeper took Yamlika
to the authorities and to his great distress, he was dragged before the governor of the
province to explain who he was.

Yamlika was asked to prove that he was a citizen of Ephesus but he could not
find anyone who knew him. Finally, a wise man from among the people spoke up
and said, "Son, there is no Emperor called Decianus. There was an Emperor of that
name living here a very long time ago, but that was long before you were born."

People were puzzled. They realized something extraordinary was going on.
Yamlika begged the officials to accompany him to the cave and finally, they
agreed to go with him.

The Emperor at that time, Theodosius II, was overjoyed at the news
of the Sleepers' miraculous awakening. He had been facing strong
opposition to the idea of resurrection and now the miracle of the
sleepers in the cave had proved that God could raise the dead. Soon
after their discovery, the young men died and the people of the
town built a place of worship at the cave where they were buried.

***God sent this sign to the people of Ephesus to show
them that He alone could raise the dead, and that
there should be no doubt over the hour of the Day
of Judgment.***

# 18 FISH

# Prophet Moses,
# Wise Al-Khidr and the Fish
### (Qur'an 18:61-64)

One day, Prophet Moses gave a very impressive sermon. All the people who heard him were deeply moved. "O Messenger of God, is there any other man on Earth more learned than you?" asked one of the listeners.

"No," answered Moses, thinking that God had given the power of miracles to him alone, and honored only him with the Torah. God soon revealed to Moses that no man could know all there is to know, nor could just one messenger be the custodian of all knowledge. There would always be another who knew what others did not know. Moses then asked God to be given a sign as to this person's identity.

"Take a live fish in a vessel filled with water. Where the fish disappears, the wise man will appear," God told him.

Moses set out on his journey accompanied by a young man who carried the vessel with the fish. When they reached the place where two seas met, they decided to stop and rest on a rock there. As soon as they sat down, Moses fell asleep.

While he slept, his servant boy watched the fish they were carrying wriggle out of the vessel into the sea and swim away. Unfortunately, he forgot to tell Moses what had happened. When

Moses woke up, the two continued on their journey until they became too tired and hungry to walk any further. "I will not give up my quest for more knowledge even if I have to spend years and years travelling," Moses told the boy. "But now we must rest and eat. Bring us our morning meal."

It was then that the servant boy remembered the fish. "The fish," he cried, "I forgot about the fish. Satan must have caused me to forget to mention it to you. It wiggled into the sea in a very strange way."

"That is the sign that we have been seeking," said Moses. And so they turned back, retracing their steps to the rock. There by the rock stood a man. They could not see him properly as the hood of his cloak partly hid his face, but they could tell by his manner that he was a saintly man. His name was Al-Khidr, and he was the knowledgeable messenger that God in His mercy had sent to Moses.

"May I follow you," Moses asked Al-Khidr, "so that you can teach me something of the knowledge and guidance given to you from God."

"You will not have patience with me," replied Al-Khidr, "for it is impossible to have patience when there are things you do not know or understand."

"If God wills it, you will find me patient and I won't disobey you," said Moses.

"Very well," Al-Khidr said, "but when something happens, don't ask me any questions about it. You must wait for me to bring up the matter with you."

They set off and everything went well, until they got into a boat. Al-Khidr started to make a hole in the bottom. "What are you doing?" asked Moses. "Are you trying to drown everybody? Surely, what you have done is an evil thing."

"Didn't I tell you that you could not be patient with me?" asked Al-Khidr calmly.

Moses apologized and said, "If I ask you anything else, please don't listen to me. I'm very sorry. I shouldn't have questioned you." Then, they continued on their journey until they met a boy. Al-Khidr killed him.

"How could you kill an innocent young man who has done nothing wrong?" asked Moses. "That's a terrible thing to do!"

"Didn't I tell you that you could not be patient with me?" asked Al-Khidr calmly Moses apologized and said, "I promise that I won't question you again, and if I do, you must walk away."

They continued on their journey until they came to a town. They asked the people of the town for some food, but the people refused them any hospitality. They walked on until they came to a wall which was about to collapse. Al-Khidr stopped and patiently rebuilt the wall. Then he set off again and Moses followed him.

"You've worked very hard rebuilding that wall," Moses called after him. "You could have asked them to pay you for that."

Al-Khidr stopped walking. "This is where we part," he said. "Now I will tell you why I did those things which you lost your patience over.

"I will start with the boat. The people who owned that boat were very poor. I made a hole in it because I knew there was a king who was seizing every seaworthy boat by force. I didn't want him to take their boat.

"As for the boy I killed – his parents were believers, and we feared that he would oppress them with his rebellion and disbelief. We intended that the Lord would send them a righteous son.

"And as for the wall, it was the property of two orphan boys in the town. Under it, there was some buried treasure belonging to them. Their father was a good man, and the Lord, in His mercy, willed them to grow to full strength and maturity before finding their treasure.

"Finally, you should know, that I did not do any of these things on my own authority. This is the interpretation of those deeds which you could not find patience for."

**Humility is its own reward.**

# 19
# SNAKES

## The Magicians and the Mighty Snake
### (Qur'an 20:20 & 7:107)

The powerful pharaoh of Egypt encouraged his citizens to look on him as a god, and the descendants of Jacob, known as the Israelites were made to work for this ruthless pharaoh for little or no money, almost as slaves, and to worship him and his idols.

One night, Pharaoh had a powerful vision, that one of the Israelites would rise up and take his throne from him. Horrified by this dream, Pharaoh commanded all male children of Israel be killed. However, because Pharaoh needed men to work for him, he ordered all baby boys to be killed every other year. Prophet Moses' mother gave birth to his brother, Aaron in the year that baby boys were spared. Unhappily, Moses was born in the year that baby boys were to be slain. God ordered Prophet Moses' mother to place him in a chest and let the chest float down the River Nile. She did this, and the chest landed at the palace of the pharaoh and it was found by his wife, the queen. Unlike her husband, the queen was God-fearing and kind. When she saw the beautiful baby boy, she decided to bring him up as her own son. She called the baby boy Moses.

Prophet Moses' sister had followed the chest to the palace. When her brother, Moses, refused to nurse from any of the women in the palace, she spoke to the queen. "I know of a woman who will be able to nurse the child," she said. The woman she spoke of was Moses' mother. And so Moses' mother came to the palace of the wicked pharaoh and she looked after her precious son. As Moses grew up, God granted him strength, knowledge and wisdom. Moses never forgot that he was an Israelite, and it made him very sad to see how cruelly the Egyptians treated his people.

One day, when Moses was in the city, he saw an Egyptian man beating an Israelite. Moses tried to help the Israelite, and not knowing his own strength, he struck the Egyptian man with a ferocious blow. The man immediately fell to the ground and died. At that time, the penalty for killing an Egyptian was death, so in fear for his life, Moses fled into the desert. He travelled in the direction of the country of Midian which lay between Syria and Egypt.

Now, Moses had left the city in a hurry so he was not prepared for a long journey. For eight days, he walked across the hot sand in the blistering heat, each new day forcing himself to continue on his journey, until finally he came to a watering hole, surrounded by shepherds and their flocks of sheep. The shepherds were jostling each other, shouting and arguing and behaving in a rowdy manner.

Exhausted, Moses slumped down under the shade of a tree, and watched the noisy shepherds. Then, he noticed two women standing back with their sheep, afraid to approach the watering hole. Forgetting his own thirst, he went over to offer his help, and he took their sheep to the watering hole for them.

That evening, the young women returned home early and their father was surprised. They told him about the kind young man they had met at the watering hole, and their father asked them to invite Moses to the house so that he could thank him personally. Moses told their father of his misfortunes in Egypt and their father invited him to stay with them. Moses accepted. One of the daughters suggested that her father asked Moses to work for him, as he was strong and trustworthy.

"How do you know he's trustworthy?" asked the father.

"When I told him to follow me home, he insisted that I walk behind him so he would not observe my form," replied the girl.

The old man was pleased to hear this and he decided Moses would be a good husband for one of his daughters. "If you will promise to work for me for eight years, I would like you to marry one of my daughters," the old man said to Moses.

Moses agreed and he married one of the girls.

After ten years living in Midian, Moses began to feel very homesick. He missed his family and he longed to return home to Egypt again. Finally

he told his wife to prepare to leave for Egypt the next day.

The next morning, they set out on their journey, and that night, as they neared Mount Tur, Moses saw a bush burning in the distance. "I'll go and fetch a burning branch so that I can light a fire here to keep us warm tonight," he told his family.

As he approached the fire, he heard a powerful voice, "O Moses, I am God, the Lord of the Universe. Throw down your staff."

Moses did as God commanded him and to his astonishment, as his staff struck the ground, it turned into a slithering snake.

"Don't be afraid," said the voice. "Pick up the snake and we shall return it to its former state." Moses picked up the snake and it became a staff again. "Now press your right hand to your left side," the voice of God said, and again Moses did as he was commanded. When he looked at his hand again, it was pure white and there was not a single blemish on it.

"You have two signs from Your Lord that He is with you. Now go to Pharaoh and his chiefs and show them these signs, for they are evil and do not live by my laws," said God.

However, Moses was afraid that if he went to Pharaoh, he would be executed because he had killed a man. God promised that he would protect him. Then, Moses asked if his brother Aaron could accompany him as Aaron was more eloquent, and Moses would feel stronger with him by his side.

God granted him his request. "Now go to Pharaoh," God said, "and ask him to set the Israelites free."

Prophet Moses did as God willed and he went to Egypt to see Pharaoh. "O Pharaoh, I am a messenger from the Lord of all the worlds. I come with a sign from God. You

must set the Israelites free," he said to Pharaoh.

"If you have indeed come with a sign from the Lord of all the worlds, then show me," said Pharaoh, asking Moses for proof of his prophethood.

"Very well," said Moses, and he threw his staff to the ground. It became a snake. Then he drew forth his right hand from the folds of his robe and held it up for all the onlookers to see. It was pure white, without a single blemish.

Now, at this time, there were many magicians working for Pharaoh, so he thought the snake was just another magic trick – an illusion. Pharaoh didn't want to lose his control over his people and he didn't want them to believe in any other god but himself, so he summoned his greatest magicians to the palace to take part in a contest to challenge Moses and Aaron. Moses was allowed to set the date for the contest and he chose the day of a festival which attracted citizens from all over Egypt.

That day, the streets were full of people and a large crowd gathered to watch the magicians. In the name of Pharaoh, the magicians threw their sticks and ropes to the ground and they became a sea of slithering snakes. The crowd looked on in awe. Moses was afraid, but he also felt secure in the knowledge that God would protect him and make his task easy. God directed Moses to throw his staff.

Moses' staff changed into a giant snake, and it quickly devoured all the illusionary snakes that covered the ground. The crowd cheered and shouted for Moses. The magicians were amazed. Their tricks were nothing but illusions, but Moses' snake was real. It was a sign from the one true God. They prostrated themselves, declaring their belief in the Lord of Moses and Aaron. They asked God to forgive them for the sins of magic that Pharaoh had ordered them to commit.

Pharaoh was furious and he wanted to have Moses executed immediately, but one of his family members convinced him and his council that this would not be a wise thing to do. He reminded them of what had happened to the people of Noah. Prophet Moses was not executed.

**Men make plans but God makes the best plans of all.**

# 20
# QUAILS

## Food in the Desert
### (Qur'an 20:80 & 2:57)

After the death of Joseph, a new pharaoh ruled Egypt, and he was a tyrant who oppressed the descendants of Prophet Jacob, sometimes known as the Israelites and sometimes known as the children of Israel. During his reign, this pharaoh kept the Israelites in slavery. In order to protect them, God commanded Prophet Moses and his brother Aaron to lead the Israelites out of Egypt and across the Sinai Desert to freedom. God would keep them safe on their long and difficult journey.

Moses and Aaron did as God commanded and soon they were far from civilization. As they continued south on their arduous journey across the desert, they became hungrier and hungrier, and they began to forget how difficult life had been under the pharaoh. "If only we had died in Egypt at the hands of the pharaoh," they moaned. "We were slaves in Egypt, but at least we had roast meat and fresh bread to eat. Now we have nothing. You've brought us to this desert to starve to death," they grumbled.

God heard their grumbling and He said to Moses, "Tell the people that I will give them all the food they need."

So Moses and Aaron reminded the people that it was actually God that they were grumbling about. They also assured them that God had heard their complaints. "God will give you meat to eat in the evening and all the bread you want in the morning, and every morning from now on."

That evening a large flock of quails flew over the camp. Exhausted after their long flight over the Red Sea, they fell to the ground and people ran and caught them easily with their hands. Now they had plenty to eat.

Then, the next morning, after the dew had gone, the Israelites found the ground covered with white flakes like snow. When they saw it, they asked each other, "What is it?" For they did not know what it was.

Moses said, "This is the bread which God has sent for you to eat." It was round and white like pale pearls and as sweet as honey to taste. The Israelites called it manna. They gathered it up and ate it like bread.

However, instead of being grateful for the food that God had provided, they continued to complain. They had not had to work hard for this food, but still they were not happy and they wanted more. God said, they did Him no wrong but only wronged their own souls.

God says in the Holy Qur'an, "O children of Israel, We delivered you from your enemy (Pharaoh). We made a covenant with you on the right side of Mount Sinai and We sent down to you manna and quails."

*For the benefit of our souls, we should be grateful*
*to God for all that He provides.*

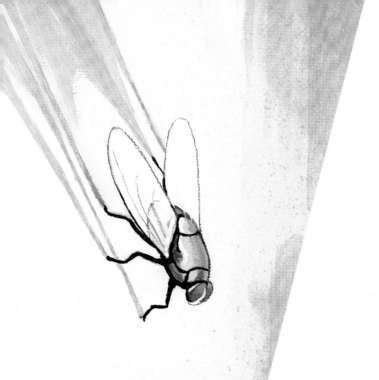

# 21
# FLIES

## (Qur'an 22:73)

Omankind! Listen to this! Any deities you call on other than God, would never even be able to create a fly, even if all of them were to come together for that sole purpose!

And if a fly should snatch anything from them, they would have no power to retrieve it from the fly. Weak are those who call, and weak are those to whom they call!

*If God does not will it, arrogant is he who believes he can create even a fly without the help of God.*

# 22
# ANTS

## Prophet Solomon and the Ants
### (Qur'an 27:16-19)

God loved Prophet Solomon and his father Prophet David, peace be upon both of them. God gave them both great wisdom and allowed Solomon to inherit his father's throne. He was a just and wise ruler.

One other gift given to this prophet, that was not given to any other prophet, before or after him, was the ability to understand the languages of animals, birds, insects and jinns. There are many stories which tell of this special talent of his. This particular story, however, is about Solomon and the ants.

One day, whilst out commanding his forces of jinns, humans, animals and birds, Solomon and his great army marched into a valley where there were ants.  On seeing the mighty army, and realizing that its soldiers might crush them unintentionally, a wise ant cried out to her fellow ants, "Everybody run back to your nests immediately. King Solomon and his army might accidently trample on us."

Solomon heard the tiny creature and he smiled at her words. Then, quickly he commanded his soldiers to tread carefully so that not one innocent ant would be trampled underneath their rough feet.  This noble prophet also thanked Almighty God for granting him the skill of understanding the language of insects and for saving the ants' lives.

**We must love and respect all God's creatures no matter how small they are.**

# 23
# THE HOOPOE BIRD

## How Prophet Solomon Met the Queen of Sheba
### (Qur'an 27:20-44)

Prophet Solomon was a wise and just king and he wanted the best for his kingdom and his people. Once, whilst travelling through Yemen, he noticed the clever irrigation system used to channel water through the cities, and he was very impressed.

Solomon was keen to build a similar irrigation system in his own country but he did not have enough springs. He would need to find a good underground source of water. Fortunately, he knew that amongst his army of birds, animals and insects, there was a special bird called the hoopoe bird, which could help him. God had blessed Solomon with a very special gift. He could communicate with the animals, the birds and the insects. That day, Solomon sent signals everywhere to find the hoopoe, but it was nowhere to be found. "I hope that bird has a good reason for its absence, or it will be severely punished," he declared angrily.

Eventually, the hoopoe came to Solomon and explained the reason for its absence. "I come from Sheba (modern-day Ethiopia and Yemen) and I have some very important news for you," said the hoopoe.

Solomon's anger was swiftly replaced by curiosity. "Tell me what you've found."

"Sheba is ruled by a queen called Balqis who is blessed with plenty, including a splendid throne," said the hoopoe. "But in spite of all her wealth, Satan has entered her heart and the hearts of her people. I was shocked to learn that they worship the sun instead of God the Almighty. They have no guidance."

Prophet Solomon decided to send a letter to the queen. "Take this letter to the Queen of Sheba," he told the hoopoe. "Once she has the letter, hide and watch her as she reads it."

The hoopoe bird did as Prophet Solomon asked. He flew swiftly to Sheba. Once at the palace, he swooped down and dropped the letter in the queen's lap as she sat on her magnificent throne. Then he flew away and hid.

"Who could this letter be from?" Excitedly, the queen opened the letter and read it. 'In the Name of God, the Most Beneficent, the Most Merciful: do not defy me, but come to me as true believers who submit to God.'

The queen was disturbed by this and hurriedly summoned her advisors to ask for their advice. They saw the letter as a challenge. "This is from a noble King hinting at war and our defeat. He means to defeat us and make us accept his terms," they decided.

"You are wrong to think of war," the wise queen told her advisors. "Peace and friendship are more beneficial than war. War only brings humiliation. It enslaves people and destroys all that is good," she continued. "No, I will not go to war with King Solomon. Instead, I will send him gifts. Yes, I'll send him some of our most precious treasures. The courtiers who deliver these gifts will have an opportunity to learn about this powerful King and his military might."

King Solomon's men informed him in advance of the arrival of the Queen of Sheba's envoys bearing gifts. He understood immediately that the queen had sent her men on a mission to find out how strong his army was. Quickly, he gave orders to rally the army.

The queen's envoys watched King Solomon surveying his army, and they were surprised by the number and variety of soldiers. They were even more surprised to find that the army included lions, tigers and birds amongst its ranks. They stood in awe, before this unconquerable force.

Eagerly, the envoys presented the Queen of Sheba's precious gifts and told King Solomon that the queen wished him to accept these gifts as an act of friendship.

King Solomon thanked them but he didn't even ask for the containers carrying the gifts to be opened. "God has given me plenty of wealth. He has given me a large kingdom and prophethood," he said. "I don't need these gifts. My only objective is to spread the belief in the one true God." He then directed them to take the gifts back to the queen. "Tell her that if she does not stop her worship of the sun, I will invade her Kingdom and drive its people from the land."

The queen's envoys returned to Sheba with the gifts and delivered King Solomon's message. They also told her of the beauty of his kingdom and the might of his army. Instead of taking offence, the queen decided to visit Solomon. Accompanied by her royal officials and servants, she left Sheba, and sent a messenger ahead to inform Solomon that she was on her way to meet him.

Solomon asked the jinns in his employment if any of them could bring her throne to the palace before she arrived. "I will bring it to you before this sitting is over," replied one. The King said nothing. The jinns competed with one another to please him, each promising to bring the throne sooner than the others.

"I will bring it here to you in the twinkling of an eye!" said another, who had the Knowledge of the Book. No sooner had this jinn spoken, than the queen's throne appeared before them, two thousand miles away from its home in Sheba. This was indeed a great miracle. "My Lord has sent this to me to test me. He wants to see if I will give thanks or show no gratitude," said Solomon. "Disguise the throne and let's see if the queen is guided to see the truth and recognizes it or she is one of those who refuse to believe."

When the Queen of Sheba arrived at King Solomon's palace she was welcomed with all the pomp and ceremony befitting a great queen. As they walked into the assembly hall, Solomon pointed to the queen's throne. "Do you recognize this throne?" he asked.

The queen stared at the throne. She knew that it could not possibly be her throne because that was at home in her palace, yet this throne did bear a striking resemblance to hers. "It looks like my throne," she replied. "In fact, it resembles it in every respect." Solomon could see by her answer, that she was both wise and diplomatic.

King Solomon invited her into the great hall as his honored guest. The floor was inlaid with crystal which shimmered like the still waters of a vast lake. Thinking it was water, the queen lifted her skirt slightly as she stepped onto it. Solomon said it was made of crystal. "I've never seen such a thing before," she said.

The queen realized that she was in the company of a very wise man, who was not only the ruler of a great kingdom but was also a messenger of God. She recognized him as a prophet. She stopped her worship of the sun and accepted the faith of God instead, and she asked her people to do the same.

*There is no god but God. He is above His creation.*

# 24
# SPIDERS

## (Qur'an 29:41)

Those people who ask false gods to protect them and give them shelter rather than asking God, are like the spider who spins itself a web as a home. The spider has no idea that its web is the frailest of all houses. The web offers the spider no protection from the heat or the cold, the wind or the rain.

***Only God can offer true protection.***

# 25
# TERMITES

## The Death of Prophet Solomon
### (Qur'an 34:14)

Prophet Solomon was the only prophet to whom God gave the ability to communicate with the jinns, which are unseen creatures made from smokeless flames of fire. Unfortunately the jinns claimed that they could see the unseen and that they could also see the future, and at that time, the old pagan Arabs believed this. God helped Prophet Solomon to prove to people that the jinns didn't have this ability.

In the year 924 BC, Solomon commanded the jinns to build him a temple and they set to work.

While the jinns were working very hard, God caused Prophet Solomon to die silently whilst standing leaning on his cane. Everybody, including the jinns thought he was still alive, and so the jinn's continued to build the temple.

God ordered a termite to weaken the cane by slowly gnawing its way through the wood. Suddenly, the cane gave way and the body of Prophet Solomon fell to the ground.

Prophet Solomon had prayed to God, that when he died, the jinns would not know about his death. He knew that they would stop working immediately, and the temple they were building would not be completed. He didn't want that to happen. So when Prophet Solomon fell to the ground, it was made clear to the jinns and to everybody else, that jinns couldn't see the future or the unseen, because if they had, they would not have continued to build the temple.

**Only God knows everything.**

# 26
# SHEEP

## Prophet David and the Quarrel over a Ewe
### (Qur'an 38:21-25)

Have you heard the story of the two quarrelling men?  They climbed over a wall into Prophet David's private chambers.

When they entered the presence of Prophet David, he was greatly alarmed.  In fact, he was scared.

"Don't be afraid!" said one.  "We've had a disagreement.  One of us has been unfair to the other.  You must decide now which of us is in the wrong.  Be truthful and treat us justly.  Guide us onto the right path."

"This man is my brother," said the other.  "He has ninety-nine ewes, and I have only one, yet he says I should give her into his care and he tells me this in a harsh tone of voice."

"Your brother has undoubtedly wronged you in demanding that you give him your only ewe to be added to his large flock," said Prophet David.  "In truth, many partners in business wrong each other, except for those who believe, and act honestly and honorably, but they are few and far between."

Prophet David understood that God had tested him.  The quarrelling men disappeared, as quickly as they had appeared.  This noble prophet then asked forgiveness from his Lord.  He prostrated himself and turned to God in repentance.

*There are always two sides to every story and it is best to hear both sides in their entirety, in order to judge wisely.*

# 27
# HORSES

## Solomon's Horses and the Winds
### (Qur'an 38:31-33)

After his father King David died, Prophet Solomon became king. He prayed to God to give him a kingdom greater than that of anybody before or after him, and God granted his wish. Besides wisdom, God had blessed Solomon with many abilities. He could command the winds and he could understand and talk to birds, animals and insects.

God directed him to teach both men and jinns to mine the earth and extract its minerals to make tools and weapons.

Solomon had a great army and horses were an important part of his army. They were essential for defense in wartime. The animals were well cared for and well trained.

One day, Prophet Solomon was viewing a parade of his horses. The fitness, beauty and posture of the horses fascinated him so much that all time was forgotten. He stayed with the horses, stroking and admiring them until the sun had nearly set and the time for the afternoon prayer (Asr) had passed. It made our noble Prophet Solomon very sad that he had missed the prayer. He was a very obedient worshipper of God and always asked His forgiveness. This time was no exception. "My Lord forgive me and bestow upon me a kingdom such as shall not belong to anyone after me," he said.

God was pleased that Prophet Solomon had asked for forgiveness. He granted Prophet Solomon the ability to control the winds, which on his command, blew gently wherever he willed. God also granted him control of the devils among the jinns, and every kind of builder and diver (to extract precious stones from the sea), and slaves as well.

"This is our gift to you, so spend it or withhold it. No account will be asked," God said to Prophet Solomon.

Prophet Solomon enjoyed a special closeness to God and a return to Paradise.

**To those who seek forgiveness, God is most merciful.**

# 28
# HUMAN BEINGS

### (Qur'an 38:71-85)

When God first made a human being, He breathed His spirit into him. The spirit of knowledge and the will, which if correctly used, would give human beings superiority over all other creatures.

"Behold!" God said to the angels. "I am about to create a man from clay. When I have fashioned him satisfactorily and have breathed My spirit into him, fall down in obedience to him." So all the angels prostrated themselves before Adam. That is all the angels except for Iblis, (Satan).

He was too proud and he only saw the inferior side of the man. He was just something made of clay. Iblis refused to see his superior side, the spirit that God had breathed into him.

Iblis was one of the disbelievers.

"O Iblis, what prevents you from prostrating yourself before one whom I have created with My own hands?" God asked him. "Are you too proud or are you already among the eminent and the powerful?"

"I am better than Adam," said Iblis. "You created me from fire and You created him from clay."

Iblis disobeyed God, and he was banished from Paradise. "Then leave," said God, "for you are expelled, and My curse shall be upon you until the Day of Judgment!"

"O my Lord, give me a period of respite, until the day the dead are resurrected," said Iblis.

"Very well, you will be one of those whose punishment is postponed until the Day of Judgment," replied God.

"By Your might, I will surely mislead them all," said Iblis, "except for those among them, who are Your chosen servants."

"Then as truth is My oath, and I speak only the truth," replied God. "I will definitely fill Hell with you (Iblis) and all those who follow you, every single one of them."

*God's servants, sincere and purified by His grace, will have no fear, nor will they grieve on the Day of Judgment.*

# 29
# LIONS

## (Qur'an 74:51)

'What, then, is the matter with them that they turn away in aversion from the Reminder (the Qur'an), as though they were frightened wild donkeys, fleeing from a lion?' (Qur'an 74:49-51)

In the Holy Qur'an, God only makes one reference to lions. This and the preceding verse show how on the Day of Judgment, the disbelievers will look like wild donkeys fleeing from a pursuing lion.

***Obey God so that you do not have to fear or grieve on the Day of Judgment.***

# 30
# MOTHS

## (Qur'an 101:4)

On the Day of Judgment when every human being will be raised up to appear before the Lord, people will be like scattered moths fluttering about. Some will feel helpless, especially those who did not obey God during their lifetime. They will run here and there like fluttering moths, suddenly exposed to a bright light.

*Be grateful that you have been forewarned of this imminent event.*

# 31
# ELEPHANTS

## The Year of the Elephant
### (Qur'an 105:1-5)

Prophet Muhammad, may the peace and blessings of God be with him, was born around the year 570 AD in what is known as the year of the elephant.

The House of God was originally built by Prophet Adam, the first man, then it was washed away in the flood in Prophet Noah's time. After that, it was rebuilt by Prophet Abraham and his son Ishmael in the barren valley of Mecca. Because it looks like a cube, this very special house was called the Ka'ba, which means cube. For many years people would come to visit this house to worship God. The area of holy land surrounding Mecca and the Ka'ba was considered a sanctuary or a safe place where no one was allowed to harm an animal, an insect or even a blade of grass. This area was known as the Haram. If anyone wanted to fight, they had to travel outside the Haram to do so.

Further south, in Yemen, there lived a man called Abraha Al-Ashran. He was the governor of Yemen and he was a Christian. Abraha knew that long ago Yemen, his home country, had once been a wealthy and important country.

In fact, in the time of Prophet Solomon, Yemen was called Sheba and it was ruled by the beautiful Queen Balqis. Abraha, an ambitious man, was jealous of the love the Arabs had for the Ka'ba. He wanted to build a house of worship so magnificent that the Arabs wouldn't want to go to the Ka'ba any more. Instead they would come to Yemen and bring their money

with them. "Yemen will be wealthy again," he thought.

And so Abraha set out to build the most splendid and most beautiful cathedral in the region, using marble taken from the ruins of the palace of the Queen of Sheba. He placed crosses of gold and silver within the cathedral and built pulpits of ebony and ivory inside. It was a truly magnificent sight. When it was finished, Abraha wrote to King Negus and described to him the wonderful cathedral he had built in his kingdom. "No other kingdom has such a beautiful cathedral," Abraha boasted to all who would listen to him. This cathedral was named Al-Qullais.

The Arabs however still preferred to worship God at the Ka'ba. This made Abraha even more jealous. Unfortunately, Abraha's boasting angered some of the Arabs, and one man from the tribe of Banu Kinanah did something terrible. He went to Yemen one night and defiled the cathedral that Abraha had built. Then, he made his way quickly to the safety of his home and his tribe.

On seeing this, Abraha was angry beyond words. He didn't look for the culprit and ask him to clean up the mess or pay for the damage. He didn't even visit the leaders of the tribe of Kinanah. Instead, Abraha decided to seek revenge! He was set on destroying the Ka'ba! "Once it's destroyed," he thought, "the Arabs will be forced to come to Yemen and with them will come their money." Yemen would be rich and glorious once again.

Abraha gathered together a powerful army, the largest army anyone had ever seen in those times, and he placed at its front the greatest and the mightiest beast of all – an elephant. This elephant's name was Mahmud. The Arabs' camels, horses, donkeys and mules were no match for this powerful elephant. No Arab army could stop them. As Abraha advanced north on his journey, he grew even bolder. Along the way, he plundered whatever riches he could, and he stole as many as two hundred camels. Now, the camels he stole belonged to a very special man called Abdul Muttalib. Abdul Muttalib was the grandfather

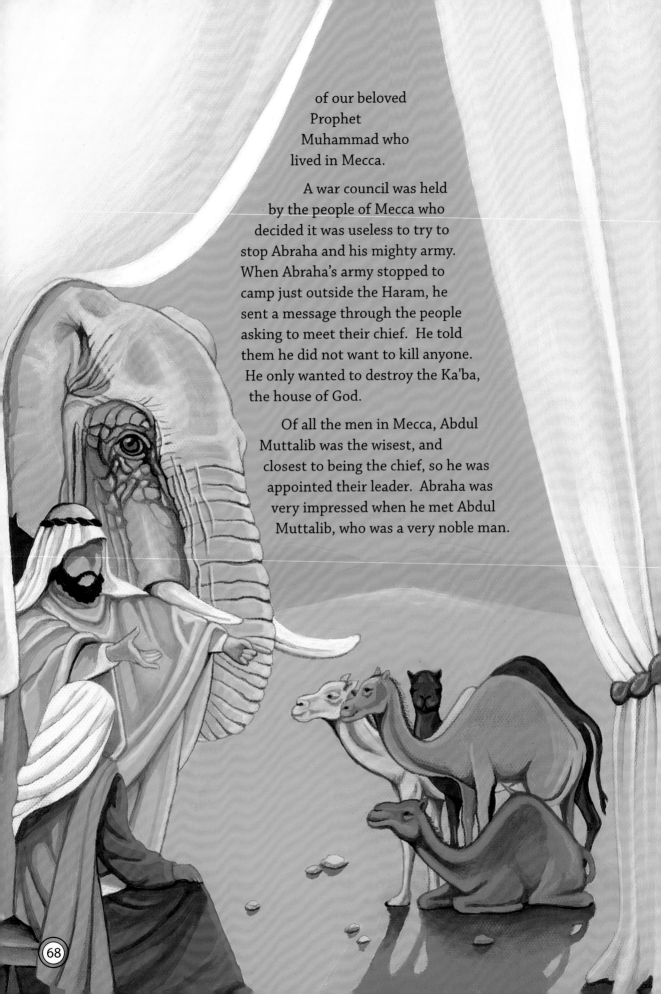

of our beloved Prophet Muhammad who lived in Mecca.

A war council was held by the people of Mecca who decided it was useless to try to stop Abraha and his mighty army. When Abraha's army stopped to camp just outside the Haram, he sent a message through the people asking to meet their chief. He told them he did not want to kill anyone. He only wanted to destroy the Ka'ba, the house of God.

Of all the men in Mecca, Abdul Muttalib was the wisest, and closest to being the chief, so he was appointed their leader. Abraha was very impressed when he met Abdul Muttalib, who was a very noble man.

During their conversation, Abraha asked Abdul Muttalib if he wanted any favors from him.

"I would like you to return my camels," said Abdul Muttalib.

"When I first met you, I was so impressed by you, that I thought even if you had asked me to withdraw my army and go back to Yemen, I would have done that," said Abraha. "But now I have no respect for you. You could have saved your precious house of worship, the Ka'ba, but instead you have asked me to return your camels."

"I am the owner of the camels, and so I tried to save them. God is the Owner of this sacred House and He will protect it," replied Abdul Muttalib.

Abraha was surprised by Abdul Muttalib's reply but he agreed to give him back his camels. Then, Abdul Muttalib went to the people of Mecca and warned them to leave the city and head for the surrounding hills. Next, Abdul Muttalib went to the Ka'ba and prayed to God for help. The very next day, Abraha marched his troops towards Mecca. Just as they reached that invisible boundary that marked the sanctuary around Mecca (the Haram), a man called Nufayl Bin Habib, a war captive, who was acting as a guide, pulled Mahmud the elephant's ear. "Kneel, Mahmud!" he said. "Kneel. Then turn around and go back home safely. You are in God's sacred city."

Mahmud kneeled down and refused to move forward towards the Ka'ba. The soldiers stuck their spears into him and hit him but he would not move. The wiser men in Abraha's army knew this was a bad omen. Abraha, however, was still determined to attack and destroy the Ka'ba. His soldiers tried to trick the elephant. They turned him towards Yemen, and he stood up. But when he was turned back towards the Ka'ba, he knelt down again and refused to move.

In the west, the sky grew black. The darkness crept closer and closer and with it came the cawing sound of a flock of birds. Suddenly, the air was filled with small birds, each armed with bullets of baked clay the size of chickpeas, one in each beak and one in each claw. As these heavenly birds swooped down on Abraha's army, they let go of their clay bullets and they hit the soldiers with such force that they pierced their coats of armor and went straight through their bodies. Almost all the wounded men died there or on their difficult journey back to Yemen. Abraha was severely wounded too and he died on the way back to Yemen.

God spared the elephant, Mahmud from harm, as well as some of the men who had been captives of war or forced to come along against their will. Those men stayed in Mecca, which they made their home, and they became shepherds.

Fifty days after God had defeated Abraha, a grandson was born to Abdul Muttalib. The baby was named Muhammad, a name never heard before, but often heard since. It means someone worthy of praising. Forty years later, the baby Muhammad became Prophet Muhammad.

**God is above all His creation.**